the flap pamphlet series

Candy Coated Unicorns and Converse All Stars

open, read, turn

Candy Coated Unicorns and Converse All Stars

the flap pamphlet series (No. 2)
Printed and Bound in the United Kingdom

Published by the flap series, 2011
the pamphlet series of flipped eye publishing
All Rights Reserved

Cover Design by Petraski
Series Design © flipped eye publishing, 2010
Author Photo © Naomi Woddis

First Edition
Copyright © Inua Ellams 2011

A fist bump to editors and staff of the following publications for publishing poems (and previous versions of the poems) in this book: Portrait of Prometheus as a Basketball Player (Salt Book of Younger Poets 2011 - Salt), Corrine Bailey Rae (City State – Penned in the Margins), Of all the Boys of Plateau Private School (Salt Book of Younger Poets 2011), Leather Comets (Literary Dundee), Class Zero (Wasafiri), Clubbing (Untitled – Oberon, City State – Penned in the Margins, Creativ Africa), Candy Coated Unicorns and Converse All Stars (Poetry for Lebanon, Jupiter), Lilly and the Lady Bird (Jupiter), Glass Xylophones and Vastness (Poetry Paper, Magma), Twenty Five (Creativ Africa), Dear Tina (Pen International), Guerilla Garden Writing Poem (Salt Book of Younger Poets 2011 - Salt, City State – Penned in the Margins, Untitled - Oberon), Lovers, Liars, Conjurers and Thieves (Night Time, Pen Pusher Magazine)

ISBN-13: 978-1-905233-33-5

LOTTERY FUNDED

Candy Coated Unicorns and Converse All Stars

This is *still, still* dedicated to capsules of walking water
- sculpted by the wind.

Inua Ellams

Contents | *Candy Coated Unicorns and Converse All Stars*

Candy Coated Unicorns 7

Portrait of Prometheus as a Basketball Player 8
Corinne Bailey Rae...9
Fragments of Bone 11
Of All the Boys of Plateau Private School, ...14
Leather Comets 17

and 21

Class Zero..22
Clubbing..24
Candy Coated Unicorns & Converse All Stars................26
Lilly and the Ladybird 29
Glass Xylophones and Vastness...32

Converse All Stars 33

Twenty Five...34
Dear Tina, ...36
Directions 37
GuerrillaGardenWritingPoem 39
Lovers, Liars, Conjurers and Thieves................................41

Candy Coated Unicorns

Portrait of Prometheus as a Basketball Player

His layup starts from mountains
not with landslide, rumble or some gorgon clash
of titans, but as shadow-fall across stream –
some thief-in-the-night-black-Christ
type stealth. In the nights before this,
his name, whispered in small circles, muttered
by demigods and goddesses, spread rebellious,
rough on the tongues of whores and queens,
pillows pressed between thighs, moaning.
Men will call him father, son or king
of the court. His stride will ripple oceans,
feet whip-crack quick, his back will scar,
hunched over, a silent storm about him.
Both hands blurred, scorched, bleeding;
you see nothing but sparks splash off
his palms, hear nothing but breeze beneath
his shuck 'n' jive towards the basket
carved of darkness, net of soil and stars.
Fearing nothing of passing from legend to myth,
he fakes left, crossover, dribbles down
the line, soars - an eagle chained
to hang time.

Corinne Bailey Rae

Maybe her voice isn't sky-borne or drifting,
instead, a captured clasp of earth spirit, an orchid
of the valley or some kindred of hymns. For music
comprehension is a varied thing; as words only
grasp at meaning, chords try to clasp mood -
it calls interpretation and all answers are true.

The hi-fi plays this newly favoured tune,
speakers spawn sound waves. I climb baselines
like ladders, notes like rungs, climb till nestled,
centering the song, waft through window now wood,
keys and wings - a human amplifier audio-colouring
the wind. Internalising, I become the full song;

the guitarist's fingertips pressed against nylon,
the gentle roar of a drum, a tired lion unwinding
in the Serengeti of strings. The baseline dwindles,
song fades, and dropped noise naked, barefooted
off-beat, note how quiet, how still lies the street.

No rival music. No bullying beat. Not the mischief
magic of children scurrying, whatever else moves
does so discreet. It's tumble-weed from a Texan
desert and this street holds guns and outlaws,
how the Wild West way fits the clear morning!

I climb through the window, pull the blinds shut
save a light beam that tingles, touching corners
growing bold; by its brightness, a pattern unfolds.

The beam hits a tumbled glass and scatters,
the glass plays prism, a rainbow pallet splatters
and colours come into their own, red rides an apple,
bleeds into a burning candle's orange glow, wax
drips onto a copy of *Othello*, the yellow'd paper
greens where blue ink stains, fades to a dusty
indigo, rests on a violet folder.

This harmonious violent, accidental rainbow
hits a mirror and smatters across the room, sends
a thousand things twinkling in the summer gloom.
A confined borealis blinks, sinks into the swirl
and soft madness of a still warm duvet: the ghost
of sleep rises to meet the ghost of music, entwines
in the sparse sparkle. Worn footpaths in the carpet
look like crop circles, and a natural mystic fills the air.

In this jigsaw puzzle devised by one far diviner
than I, I am the piece where the mountain peak
meets the sky; the silence-amplifying skin prism
reforming the light, who fits within the ceiling,
blue walls and floor boards.

I wonder, if in someplace other, a mile from here,
similar room, similar clutter, maybe a browner shade
of blue, someone kneels: head in the clouds, body
in a valley of hymns, listens to Corinne's captured
clasped spirit and wonders about fitting in?

Fragments of Bone

Let me begin again, I say, as the bar blurs
invisible, its volume reduced to the merest
suggestion of others and it's just us spotlit
in the black womb-like silence of theatre
and your question themes the play; let me
begin again: I went to church last Sunday.

The pastor preached: put not your faith in
man who only is good as his next breath;
align your faith with he who gives breath.
Here I stutter, my answer splintering like
fragments of bone against the mud soil
of memory. Moments before, I recalled

the call to prayer: In the Name of Allah
Most Gracious, Most Merciful – the slow
unfurling Imam's son's voice as dusk
touched the courtyard, the dust settling,
the sun solemnly bowed on the horizon –
thin as a prayer mat – and the gathered
performing ablutions: Bismillah, they say,
washing hands, mouths, nostrils, faces,
arms, head, ears, feet, kneeling to pray
Allah Is Great, God Is Great, they say.

You counter with airplanes, fireballs,
towers falling; stop your rant with
the first fireman to die, his skull caved

by a jumper from the 51st floor fleeing
flames. In the name of Allah, Gracious,
Great, Merciful this was done, you say.

I mention Amazing Grace, how sweet
the choir leader swayed in white robes,
eyes closed, humming southern baptist
hymn hypnotic, sailing congregations
to the oceanic depth whence his tears:
wide and sure as waves ride back and
forth that everything would be all right.

You reject faith again, describing Jos,
Nigeria, the girl watching flat amongst
tall grass: the squad of Christian men
who hold her mother down as another
swings down with a machete, down as
sunlight skates the blade's edge, down,
the last swing, the fragments of bone
and there are screams no more.

There's blood in the drama of Men and
Gods, you say: rivers of it flow through
our wounded earth, gush from scripts
in houses of worship and act after act
aren't all stained? except the audience?
the secular astray? You gesture toward
those seated in darkness who gawk as we
squabble on stage; aren't they the ones
the light beyond will touch unbloodied?
who will die hands clean?

… Let me begin again, I say, I went to church/the pastor preached/faith/man /breath/… I stutter, the bar blurs back to life, words falls against your ears.

Of All the Boys of Plateau Private School,

the dry skinned short shorted dust-dipped
disciples of Bruce Lee and Chuck Norris,
of all the wire headed heathen, my posse

of Voltron-Forced, Fragle-Rocked, Teenage
Mutant Hero Nerds each had a party trick.
Kika B would eat a fist-full of desert sand

spiced with soldier ants, chew till it turned
the beige mulch of Rich Tea biscuits,
swallow twice, and live to tell the tale.

Dapo Mokoye could flatulate the first line
of the national anthem with such clarity,
Raymond Ogunsayo swore he heard words.

T could spit faster than fleas skip, further
than lizards leap, spit so high, we claimed
him herculean in form, a half-god of rainfall

and of the four talents, I was the art kid

awaiting the school bell. With the sun for
floodlights, the ground for canvas, a sharp
twig splashing sand about like paint,

I'd capture Kika's grin, Dapo's musical sin,
T's thick lips saliva dripping and me, angled

as a Ghetto van Gogh - shoulders hunched
to get the staunch slouch right. We'd pose

beside the drawing, sculptures of ourselves,
the other boys clustered, dark eyed, envious
but not enough to scatter sand in any way.

So this day after, we sidle into school, still
sketch-slouched, find our canvas suddenly
blank, sand - mysteriously smoothed...

Most likely the janitor simply did his job,
but instead we imagine creatures of
the night, voodoo priests and priestesses,

mami waters, bush babies, witch doctors,
sorcerers, all the sulphur-scorched-glowing
-eyed-black-circled venom stuff rumoured

to work the night, we theorise they spent
their witching hour playing with our sand.
The priest outlined us in white chalk, spoke

in voodoo talk, raised up dust dolls of us
who, naked with the witches, limboed
with their brooms; bush babies gaggled

and gooed in devil-glee till the clock struck
three, they vanished instantly, a foul wind
of howling wolves swept through, leaving

sand smooth as fresh sheets, as the wide

ruled page I dent and reminisce of tongues
turned tireless, of dark art's thrill, of how
quick we fixed our lil' plight with fantasy

which flows, you know, ever shapes, ever
reveals the world - an unquenchable sea of
myth-mist that wisp-whips whoever asks it

some trap it with tongues or a double bass
strummed, some turn its incline to sculpted
forms, a boy once enticed it with sand and
a stick or now, as I do, with a pad and a Bic.

Leather Comets

If you didn't see our hands on fire it doesn't matter. The backboard
bears the burn marks, the rim remembers heat. As for skin, we learnt to
play without it /

I remember the sky, bright orange clouds arranged in the scattered
ordered causality of the cosmos. Beneath, walking to the sports courts
with a bag and a basketball were five boys, the starting school team. On
the far left, Gary, point guard, a geek so boring he'd attempt to calculate
the trajectory of a shot before scoring. By him fared Cullen, nicknamed
'*FatBoy*'. Though built average and so spanned his chest, always he
was eating, jaws never seemed to rest. On the far right abreast walked
Wesley, the widest / strongest of we ball drones. Beside his barrel
biceps and muscles toned walked O.B. the smallest soft-spoken one /

Normally, boisterous would be we boys: we jump shooting / no-blows-
pulling boys. Instead, stilled lay the labour of noise, no sound from we
slouched hands-pocketed boys and the reason lay middled in that day /

I remember the school grounds, but forget its name, remember the
sickly speckled painted hallway. Away games always made us feel
nauseous, this was no different; remember how parched the ball court
seemed, how the four gym walls seemed close to bursting in as though
walls were dams with oceans pressing in. So I sensed the pressure
but disbelieved the leaking, disbelieved the resentment-river rushing
in. The front row started the sea rolling, sent the entire auditorium
into frenzied name-calling. We five, capsized by the sewage of the
sea, swam for land as the storm sang with *go back to Africa*, voices
unrelenting as a wave's ride /

Against the rising tide, Gary life boated *don't listen*, drowning I replied *Gary, this is no thing for I know no niggers / I know no coons / know neither monkey / jungle bunny / nor baboon / I've waded deeper waters, Gary, these leave no wounds.* Came the final whistle, we'd conceded the game. Worsening the flooding and a fall from grace were my boys, feeling embarrassed, couldn't look at my face /

Gary, stiff in his glass frames wore a cold blue gaze. Cullen cursed in the way only the Irish know. Wesley cried, this, the hardest of all to hold, those great shoulders quaking, inconsolable, absurd O.B. sat stone silent / no movement / no word. But I say, in stone silence lies the sharpest sword sheathed. We five, my four kindred and I were a sight sorried by an afternoon so horrid we feared the future's yield. At the dry courts back in our home field, still the silence persisted. Only a forced score of syllables passed between us - five boys embarrassed in their own skin /

O.B. the soft speaker, still vexed by the drama, withdrew the basketball, searched the bag for a can of deodorant, sprayed it with Lynx, unleashed a lighter and lit it. The ball burst into flames passed to Wez who screamed like a girl, let fly a right hook and hit it to Gary, who true to stoic form, caught the fire, mastered the pain, felt a gasp rising to his tongue - bit it (and from our lost voices swift came this giant game of hot potato, the point being to score - one point) swung to Cullen cross backed to me. I heel spun and swung back to O.B. who sharp, sure as a stone sheathed sword, rocked back without a word /

And I remember the leather ball aflame - now localized comet sailing, the most fragrant fire trails tailing its arch towards the hoop. Beneath that leather star, sensed a joining of we star gazers, a twenty limbed creature of mixed culture and race, palms burnt united by this stunt / this state / of being one, watching the basketball comet commence a crescendo - buffering the jostling of adolescent release, our lungs were closed caskets of cries awaiting the *swish* sound signal for freedom /

A minute later, our hands cooled under a tap. The simple wetness was a baptism from fire, the twenty limbed creature became five boys again, underwater, our fingerprints were growing, interrupted by the oohs / aahs / laugher of victory, sowing sentiments, the sanctity of this game saved /

If you didn't see our hands on fire, it doesn't matter. The backboard bears the burn marks, the rim remembers heat. As for skin, we learnt to play without it /

and

Class Zero

Double class after lunch is maths lesson. I walk in impeccably dressed
in uniform till James Cannon, my best friend, whose wit is swift as
comets, announces to the class: "Inua has a minus area" - that's the
mathematical term for a black hole. I jump over the table, grab James
in a headlock, grind my knuckles into the crown of his skull till his
knees buckle. He screams, calling others into our mock scuffle and the
class becomes a mass fray, where small fists like soft rubble rain on the
buildings of our bodies -limbs like metal beams twist under the dust
clouds of voices, billow upwards and outwards, continuously /

till the maths teacher, suddenly there, pissed, calls for order. Dust
settles. In the debris of rough shirts, upturned chairs, she demands
to know the culprit of the fray. But in the calamity just passed, we've
grown together like a family of dust boys, so no one calls my name /

She shrugs and tells how ten minutes ago, two planes were flown into
the World Trade Center, calls it 'America's worst nightmare' and sinks
into a silence we take for despair. We return her news with blank stares.
We are sixteen. All we care of beyond these four walls are Pamela
Anderson / Snoop Dogg / and the tingle of taste buds before a pint of
Guinness. With no frame of reference, this is new /

I leave school puzzled, into our living room, find my father huddled
around the television, mother paces back and forth. The atmosphere
is horror laced with disbelief, I sit cross legged towards the t.v. screen,
lean into the footage played over again: two planes / crash into
buildings. Instant rubble rains off, the metal beams twist under the dust
clouds and fire, billow upwards and outwards, continuously /

till they suddenly fall. Dust settles. In the debris of torn lives and
upturned worlds, the news reader calls for the culprit of the fray, but
pauses to say how from Ground Zero, New York spawned a new race of
people - survivors of the day, concrete powdered to one tone of grey /

Years pass, I date a girl called Sara, ask what she did as the towers fell,
she say it was her birthday, she blew out her candles as the fires swelled,
the most muddled day she'd been through, I agree 'me too' /

Clubbing

It begins with shackling necklaces across throats:
the distorted custom of wearing amulets to battle
talismans to war; we are new hunters, wear jeans

for camouflage, clutch mobile phones like spears
journey to the village / town / city square, meet
the rest of the tribe – mostly in short skirts, armed

with stilettos, armoured by Chanel. Dusk thickens,
the customary bickering between us commences
through the jungle vines of power lines/stampede

of zebra crossings/night growth of streets bustling;
our ritual is natural, till the traders come. Greater
armed, they divide with such ease that most of us

are taken. Those who resist are swayed by liquor
deals, sailed to darkness where the master spins
a tune not our own. We move stiffly to it as minds

force indifference, but spines have a preference
for drums. Rage building, we make our melody,
fight to find our feet until the master tries to mix

our movement with his song… but the rhythm is
uneven and the tempo wrong. Against its waves,
we raise voices in anger, fists in protest, dancers

in the tide, militant against the music, a million
men marching through seas. But we still know
how to cross water: the ocean holds our bones,

explains our ease of navigating past bouncers
like breeze into night's air, where clouds pass
like dark ships and find us beached, benched

with parched lips, loose-limbed and looking
to light. Now, the best thing about clubbing
is not this, or the struggle to make hips sway

just so, not the need to charge cloakrooms
as if through underground railroads. No.
Best thing about clubbing is the feeling

of freedom on the ride home.

Candy Coated Unicorns and Converse All Stars

She asks what I'm crying for;
I tell her it's the same thing dolphins are dying for,
that in my last life I was ultramarinean and though
I am now a land lover, I often re-swim the blue;

These tears are re-washed waters of B.B. King's
daughters, plugged into the ocean's floor, re-sorrowed
and renewed, these tears are the blues in bloom.

I ask her what she's crying for;
shoulders slump, head rises. Bloodshot are the whites
of her eyes and her pupils sparkle bright black.
Her legs begin to buckle; I catch her before she hits
the café floor. In my arms she whispers between sobs:

it's the same thing you're crying for.
In the last hour, her boyfriend was a boxer
and her jaw will testify.

Her whole body sighs as if to speak
makes it a truth she can no longer deny
and I half-carry, half-drag her to the round table.

The café is littered with newspapers
that tell bitter fables of war in the Middle East.
Snatched snippets of its distant screams pierce
this bubble of brown water and baked yeast.

She tells of the boyfriend of a beast. As she speaks
blood drips from her broken lips, slips into her coffee cup.
Before I can stop her, she takes a sip:

it's a thing going where it should not.
I'm hoping she runs like her blood
and lets the beast be.

She holds on to this broken love, like a war
-torn mother holding to a dying child,
whose watery eyes won't let her see it's all in vain.

I squeeze her shoulders, hold her hand, say it's okay,
let it rain, we'll be here when the smoke clears:
two strangers wearing old trainers swapping tears.

A poster on the wall reads *Our deepest fear*
is not that we are inadequate,
but that we are powerful beyond measure;

we can reason faster than speeding fists,
whisper louder than atomic voices, can dream
bigger than nuclear slaps and the only excuse
that could stand is not having enough pillows
to go round. Yet we are fearful.

So in this new wasteland of coffee cups
and couches, I will be brave.

I will dare to dream a candy coated unicorn
in this bruised princess, mistake cold hot chocolate

for Kenyan beer, crunch ice cubes like frozen river water.

And when backpacks become briefcases and this table
stables wars, we will sit and converse
like all stars.

Lilly and the Ladybird

Let's say
we both paid a fiver at the door, both
despised the cloakroom's overprice till
you, shoulders crisp as new snow peaks
shivered with the dj's beats, snaked down
stairs, onto the dance floor and owned it.

Let's say
we answered the bar's call when its gin-
tingled touch stretched out to us and we
clutched the liquid fire down throats,
loosening limbs till inhibitions gave in.

I agree
after the tide of baselines we clung
to each other, knuckles white as cliffs.

But the whole -
:: record-skip/dead silence/your voice
carried over the sudden sonic void/
to land, pitch-perfect with the song ::

- that, was authored by a thing like fate,
who knew I'd fall with you to the last
note, I'd grasp close even after the echo
gave up and out to the taxi's back seat.

And how the sky, like an eye pupil'd by

the moon watched intensely, its beams
flash-lit the streets between buildings,
we slipped through shadow, then light,
then shadow, quick, cloaking the taxi
as if the sky blinked —

it knew the night would gyrate past
subtle hand clasps to your place, lights
out, tipsy but able to learn to cradle
the arch of your back, the dark breath
by hot neck, shudder, halts, hard sweat,
the formless flounder of tired sleep, to
this dawn, lifting, the sun nuzzling us.

I wake first, startled by a crash, find
Lilly, your black cat, arched over
to land on the window sill. Her paws,
a soft blur of furred lightening, streak
between two ladybirds on the glass pane.

She takes one in her mouth, drops
to the white sheet, bites into its shell,
promptly spits out the tiny carcass
and sprints, leaving this little death,
a dot of darkness that blackens the air.

I turn to you, tuck a curl of your hair
a slip of darkness, out of sight behind
your ear and watch, in the same silence
where an owl prays for prey, or one
where a puma hunts, I watch over you

frozen, frightened in the stillness,
knowing now how records always skip,
knowing fate always flows beneath and
such is darkness to bring forth beasts,

I lie there, defiant, daring them all
to mix, for a beast in the baseline
to lunge fate-spun, though it isn't ours
to know what comes, I'll watch as far
as the end of this morning, I'll stay
by your shoulder, my guard on.

Glass Xylophones and Vastness

I met a girl who met a guy who met a girl from South Dakota, who likes the thin clash of teaspoon on glass / With varying sizes she'd hazard a xylophone and last Christmas, played a medley so delicate fairy lights blinked enchanted by its rhythm /

Imagine that / an entire constellation dancing to her prancing hands / pinkies poised like tuning forks. Perhaps this came the world / a deity in darkness knocks together rocks / the aftershock and echo rocked clouds of matter / danced them human form and we are still enchanted, lives blinking on /

The guy who met that girl dives once a month / Down by the jetty where the sea spray stings he dives / not for the thick tide souping over rocks / not for the soft rock lullaby of waves / not for the seagull's brave diving / past breakwater / not for the scrawling gale / he dives beneath the surface, arms out wide and drifts to feel one with the vastness of it all /

The girl I met who met that guy is the crux of it all / You have to see her take the stage, voice husky, small / have to see her chest fall / have to note her nape shudder / gotta hear her tongue flutter the folklore of his name;

The audience hush like loosened waves / guitar strums rain / flute feigns the scrawling gale / high hats like xylophone clash us through the vastness in which we dive, which we stage / we tap out the rhythm, rage / and dance and while and age / till its enchantment tells our wage / each light, one day, blinks off /

Converse All Stars

Twenty Five

There's a Thai Food Gourmet on Horseferry Road. The walls inside are painted a warm yellow, bars tables and seats are wooden trimmed with gold. It's a place for parties: from benefits to birthdays gatherings, where such important dates are sown. Today we've claimed it made it our own. The walls are not yellow, they are sun-painted stained windows, the wood is improvised from forests where the fauna roam free, untainted. To celebrate a wedding anniversary, collected here are family members and close friends, those that'll stick together till forever ends /

The couple have been paired for twenty-five years. They know the square root of survival, how to float four children through tidal waves to safe piers. My mother is the most magnificent woman in the world, my father's words are final. His voice (an older model of mine) rises above the conjugal ensemble. He says *there are secrets to a marriage like this. Number one, the wife is always right, especially when she is wrong. Number two on the list, never let a dispute last over a day long.* He plays the part, choir-master to the chorus-like laughter of these friends in sun-rays /

In the silence after, my father thanks God for we four kids, pride bursting, in a louder tone – growing – says he'd be nothing without mother at his side. My mother hugs him, her face bright, soft, and there is a passion here, a vintage love, refined as a twenty-five year old battle-dove, body battered but stronger and sublime. I've seen beginnings of passion like this, in faces of girlfriends, in the slowed-down times. It suddenly strikes me: mother was once a girl; all short skirts and madness, a thing without a care, nothing but the Nigerian night in her hair /

The speech ends to applause and own devices. We quaff champagne, scoff cake slices. I am eating and listening as the babble rises when Rachel (sister's friend) tells me a curious thing, of a boy she gets on with; they're like fuel and fire - with them, it's almost always all flames, sapphire-furnace cuddles and ridiculous love names, says for a thing beyond her power the man is just a friend. The reason dowses fire, tames to an end, says he is from the same tribe as she is – back home, it is against tradition, it's a strict taboo for same tribe members to be as lovers should /

Neither of them dare to break the age-old custom. Surprised such a rule crossed oceans, climbed time, found these two birds and cost them their wings, I want to urge her to deny her tribe, instead, sit silenced by the sadness in her sighs. Sweeping across the tables, I see the reason why - My parents, similar customs, twenty-five years joined. Whilst such rules are ancient it has kept them strong, in truth, there are two sides to every coin. What demand holds this on future love?

Scanning the numbers for my little sister, finds all three by the Karaoke machine. Picture this: the youngest between the older other two / hands on hips / heads swing side-to-side / thrown back / lost in the spiritual sing of a tri-vocal harmonious band… They are wailing to Michael Jackson's Smooth Criminal *Annie are you okay / are you okay / are you okay Annie? /*

The moment is a monument to richness. Uncle laughs, thanks God they are in school *you'd never make it in the music business.* My sisters are spectacular (in that single-mothers-are -super-heroes sort of way), whatever future love feigns, let it come, for Mum became a little girl again and my sisters have super powers. We knowers of the way, we wave riders will find safe bays again. So Michael, on this most glorious of days, believe it, Annie is fine, Annie is okay /

Dear Tina,

The day I discovered how she survived the civil war,
how she saw her friends pass like minutes into oblivion,
how she screamed through drop zones and Morse codes
into jungle, dodging bullets, hiding and crying into rain,

the day I discovered my grandfather heard her wailing,
felt something enough to move him after her, in darkness,
through rain, how her eyes, found in the flickering bounce
of hurricane lamps, showed a place so pure, he sailed her

away to the embrace of Paris, the kiss of Rome, the world
with its wide welcoming dome. The day I discovered this,
why she called him hero, she died. Peacefully, 90 years old.
He followed an hour after, again into darkness.

All those years, he never let go. That day, I realised we live
in different worlds; friends pass too fast for minutes, wars
come after X Factor, turtle dove romances exist in the past.

But I will send one sentence to you. One text message
screaming through wifi zones, digital codes, dodging
ones and zeros, like bullets and anti-heroes, promising

if evr ur lst n ths urbn jngle,
i'll fnd n brng u in frm rain.

Directions
- after Billy Collins

You know the wild bush at the back of the flat,
the one that scrapes the kitchen window,
the one that struggles for soil and water
and fails where the train tracks scar the ground?
And you know how if you leave the bush
and walk the stunted land, you come
to crossroads, paved just weeks ago:
hot tar over the flattened roots of trees,
and a squad of traffic lights, red-eyed now
stiff against the filth-stained fallen leaves?

And farther on, you know
the bruised allotments with the broken sheds
and if you go beyond that you hit
the first block of Thomas Street Estate?
Well, if you enter and ascend, and you
might need a running jump over
dank puddles into the shaking lift
that goes no further than the fourth floor,
you will eventually come to a rough rise
of stairs that reach without railings
the run-down roof as high as you can go
and a good place to stop.

The best time is late evening
when the moon fights through
drifts of fumes as you are walking,
and when you find an upturned bin

to sit on, you will be able to see
the smog pour across the city
and blur the shapes and tones
of things and you will be attacked
by the symphony of tires, airplanes,
sirens, screams, engines –
and if this is your day you might even
catch a car chase or a hear a horde
of biker boys thunder-cross a bridge.

But it is tough to speak these things
how tufts of smog enter the body
and begin to wind us down,
how the city chokes us painfully against
its chest made of secrets and fire,
how we, built of weaker things, regard
our sculpted landscape, water flowing
through pipes, the clicks of satellites
passing over clouds and the roofs
where we stand in the shudder of progress
giving ourselves to the vast outsides.

Still, text me before you set out.
Knock when you reach my door
and I will walk you as far as the tracks
with water for your travels and a hug.
I will watch after you and not turn back
to the flat till you merge
with the throngs of buses and cyclists –
heading down toward the block,
scuffing the ground with your feet.

GuerrillaGardenWritingPoem

The mouth of the city is tongued with tar
its glands gutter saliva, teeth chatter in rail
clatter, throat echoes car horns and tyre's
screech, forging new language: a brick city
smoke-speak of stainless steel consonants
and suffocated vowels. These are trees and
shrubbery, the clustered flora battling all
hours, staccato staggered through streets.

Meet Rich and Eleanor on Brabourn Grove
as he wrestles her wheelbarrow over cobble-
stones to the traffic island by Kitto Road
where this night, coloured a turquoise-grit,
cathedral-quiet and saintly, makes prayer
of their whispers and ritual of their work:
bend over, clear rubble, cut weed and plant.

But more than seeds are sown here. You
can tell by his tender pat on tended patch;
the soft cuff to a boy's head - first day to
school, by how they rest with parent-pride
against stone walls, huff into winter's cold,
press faces together as though tulips might
stem from two lips, gather spades, forks,
weeds and go. Rich wheelbarrows back to
Eleanor's as vowels flower or flowers vowel
through smoke-speak, soil softens, the city
drenched with new language thrills and

the drains are drunk with dreams.

The sky sways on the safe side of tipsy
and it's altogether an alien time of half-
life and hope, an after-fight of gentle fog
and city smog, where the debris of dew drips

to this narrative of progress, this city tale;
this story is my story, this vista my song.
I cluster in the quiet, stack against steel
seek islands, hope, and a pen to sow with.

Lovers, Liars, Conjurers and Thieves
(An Ode to Southwark)

After five hours tied to break-beats so thick
you could bitch-slap a rapper with, rave-drunk
on bass, funk and melody, I slouch sweat-heavily
by Waterloo Bridge, ready myself to ride home.

Now, from the moment I cross over the bridge
and leave the Southbank's lights sparkling,
the River Thames, with its long lapping
happenings, hi-fives the riverside walls for me.
The road is free (usual for this hour), its silence
stars a shiver that shudders the road sign,
its flow winds by a bin bag, burst like ripe fruit,
two foxes make harvest of its juice. If you look
past their fur you'll hear the soft purr
you might've once poured into your lover's ear,
when caution thrown clear, and under shadow-
cover, were smothered in an alley with his lips.
But lovers tiff, one fox's paw fists
and their battle cries riff with the day's remnants
of torn bags, beer cans, cigarettes and spliffs.

Elephant & Castle is a coral reef, resplendent,
rippling with daredevil kids too schooled
in cool to check the pickpocket whose wrist-flick
shimmers like a blade. A shoal of girls clothed
in tinsel dresses burp and bubble with ale,
their cheap garments ripple like fish scales,
dazzling migrants sailed from a nightly slave

of mop buckets, bathrooms, broom sticks
and piss. Their tired limbs just about miss
drunk cyclists' swim cross traffic, who brake
too late, front wheels smash, chains erupt,
pedals clash, perhaps now they'll admit,
(like the rest of us) to going nowhere fast.

Camberwell is cliché hell. The bars spill out
a steady swell of weed smoke, desperate men
and willing women whose red-tipped fingers,
the same red you have cried into cold mirrors
against loneliness - that darker shade of blush,
stroke their bare arms with 'yes, my place
is yours tonight'. This same crimson rims
the eyes of dry-lipped addicts too fixed
on last fix to catch the faint wisp of endless
hope haunting a lone street lamp, whose glow
halos the crowns of boys, heads bowed low,
shoulders swaying to and fro, hands folded
to form two fingers barrelled before a cocked
thumb, this cypher's silent guns punch the air,
salute the beat-boxer's steady glare, his pressed
breath: fresh carpet, over which the MC spits
in time, conjures their lives in rhyme.

Rising; the last bastion of breath – Peckham
– rests in south's fortress. By the library, two
unmarked vans park for stop & searches.
For all their stealth, rubber-sole boots, gloves,
high powered torches; all the hours spent bent
on code names, seeking swift results to deep
problems, leads here where metal sticks choke

black throats - for all their stealth and state-
given right, they can't steal the fight from
Peckham's young, whose backs still broad,
heads so rise, skin soak shine of the new blue
moon whose dominance is fractured by
the scattered light of a firework,
out of place, but welcomed.

Close by, a barman toasts his stolen gin,
a night baby gurgles in her plastic cot,
a student pauses before a full-stop,
and the culprit strikes again:

a swift-struck matchstick blooms, the fire
works, blossoming upwards, explodes outwards,
a bouquet of sparkle fire, petalling out against
a sky, so bright it beats the sun back. Two hours
pass before it tries to climb the horizon again,
finds me hunched over by laptop screen, trying
to let my fingers know what my heart means
by this journey mashed of instances where
bin bags splash, cyclists crash, a rapper
freestyles the scene?

Well, this is how its always been, lovers, liars,
conjurers and thieves; the world is a break-beat
backed by these, over which the poets sing.

Lightning Source UK Ltd.
Milton Keynes UK
UKOW02f1033111114

241430UK00002B/57/P